Born In War: Poems of Peace Volume 1

Jamale R. Ellison

ISBN-13: 978-0692750766
ISBN-10: 0692750762

DEDICATION

First and foremost, I dedicate this book to my Lord and Savior Jesus Christ, to You be all the glory and praise! You've Lifted me from the darkest places and taught me in Your Ways, so that I may have Eternal Life.

I also dedicate this book to my wife, Olesja Ellison and my children, Julian Ellison, Ariana Ellison, and Amariah Ellison. My father, Ramish Ellison, and my mother, Irene Blanche. My grandmother, Mary Lou Ellison, as all of my brothers, sisters, and family.

I would also like to thank our Calvary Church family and friends for their continued support!

Thanks to you all for providing the inspiration.

For Tina and Jerlissa. Be at peace.

CONTENTS

BORN IN WAR: POEMS OF PEACE /VOL. I

ACKNOWLEDGMENTS

I wish to personally thank the following people for their contributions to my inspiration and knowledge and other help in creating this book:

Pastor John and the entire Calvary Church family.
Bridges Anderson and the Upward Bound Program.
1SG David Brown and the Soldiers of the 16th TIN.
All the Soldiers of the United States Military.

INTRODUCTION

As believers in Christ, we each face some form of turmoil everyday in regards to our faith. Whether it may come through our job, friends, family, or culture, there is always an enemy seeking to destroy within us that which our Lord Has Built upon us.

"Not all wars are created equal.

Some battles can't be freely seen.

These are the battles that challenge us the most in life,

These are the battles based on belief.

Though we were each born into spiritual war,

We must always remember His Grace.

Though bore in sky, and born in war,

Our lives should be as poems of peace."

The inspiration to write this book came to me during my 3rd deployment, a few days after becoming baptized in the Jordan River while in Amman. At first, I didn't understand what I was meant to do with these spiritual writings. However, through His Grace, the Lord Revealed His Purpose upon me. He Wanted me to share them with you.

It is for this reason that I write to you now my dear brothers and sisters. I pray each poems speaks to your heart and grants you inspiration through Jesus Christ. It delights me to share these writings with each of you. To Him be all glory! May GOD's Touch be upon you all.

"I stand before You broken,

But Your Will I achieve.

You Submerged me into water,

It was then that I could breathe.

You Awoke in me Your Spirit,

That is how I now proceed.

You Taught to spread Your Word,

As a dreambuilder in seed."

Jamale R. Ellison

I. POEMS OF STRENGTH

P1. "Born In War: Poems of Peace"

Poems of Strength/ J. Ellison

I. Poem I//

Apart but Together

Everyday I spend apart from you, is one moment to many.

Every word you speak through the phone, soothes me more than any lullaby I've ever known.

Every day I watch you grow through pictures posted on the Internet.

Every development, every achievement, every instant becomes my daily love drug.

Every deployment our family goes through the same song.

Every mission seeming to take us further apart, even one second is a second too long.

I rush back home at the end of the day,

Only realize you and the kids and not physically there, and still so far away.

I know you and the kids miss me greatly,

But still I wonder, my thoughts aching.

Too long away from the sound of your voice.

Too long away from the giggles of our children's laughter.

Too long away from the time of our families love and adventures again.

Too be stuck in an endless daily loop, though the end doesn't come until I truly redeploy home.

This is the single tale of all deployed Soldiers, who's love for family remains ever strong.

GOD provides each family with the strength,

Though we must remember, have faith.

We won't be apart for too long my Love, for in Him I always see your face.

P2. "Born In War: Poems of Peace"

Poems of Strength/ J. Ellison

I. Poem II//

Silent Persecution

You may,
Kick me when I'm homeless,
Punch me when my are hands tied,
Push me when I'm weak,
But destroy me never.

Some may,
Bully me while defenseless,
Target me while I visit,
Bury me in the media,
But destroy me never.

Some may slander my hometown,
Frame me when I walk straight,
Injure me when I speak truth,

But destroy me never.

Why rob me though I help you?
Laugh when I seem blue,
Step on me when I fall,
But destroy me never.

Some drag me through the mud,
Arrest me for my views,
Sensor me for my faith,
But destroy me never.

So remove me from the fight,
Even jail me for belief,
But know I walk with the Lord,
You will never destroy me..ever.

P3. "Born In War: Poems of Peace"

Poems of Strength/ J. Ellison

I. Poem III//

The Battle Cry of Hope

No one can tell you not to dream.

No one can take your dreams away from you.

No one can tell you not to become inspired.

Your dream can only become erased if you alone allow it to.

You are unstoppable!

Therefore,

Continue to dream.

Continue to inspire others.

Continue to grow as a person.

The possibilities for us all are endless.

Continue On! Continue!

GOD has wonderfully made each and everyone of you.

Let your actions become the inspiration for the next.

Let your dreams, fuel the dreamers of the future.

Let your life, become as light to others stuck in the darkness!

Go Become Great!

Visualize the outcome.

Achieve that outcome.

Conquer that mountain.

More importantly, have fun doing it.

Most importantly,

HAVE..FUN..DOING..IT!!

P4. "Born In War: Poems of Peace"

Poems of Strength/ J. Ellison

I. Poem IV//

Put It Away

We all have problems in the World,

Do not take a permanent solution to a temporary problem.

Put it away.

These seemingly major issues shall pass.

One day you will be able to look back at this situation and laugh.

Put it away.

Life throws curveballs at us all.

However, it is how we choose to respond to that pitch,

Which defines our true legacy.

Put it away.

Ignore the opinions of others.

They only seek to follow the crowd.

But you were designed to follow Greatness.

Put it away.

That terrible instant is over and behind you.

Leave it in the past, where it belongs.

Live now for the future.

Put it away.

If you could only see how much GOD truly loves you.

You'll understand there is nothing greater in life, than Life itself.

Put it away.

GOD does not make mistakes.

Therefore you were never considered as one.

Put it away.

My Child,

This moment too shall pass.

Never feel as if you are the only one.

Listen to me now.

Put it away.

For GOD is with you always.

He Adores You immensely.

There will never be another you.

You are truly one of a kind.

Yes, My Child,

I am speaking directly to you.

Now Please, Listen to me now.

Put It Away.

P5. "Born In War: Poems of Peace"

Poems of Strength/ J. Ellison

I. Poem V//

Worldly Pressure

Worldly woes may plague me,
Worldly views are against me,
Worldly thoughts fight within me,
But I will not budge.

Worldly laws may ban me,
Worldly songs may taunt me,
Worldly movies may mock me,
But I will not budge.

Worldly talk condemns me,
Worldly families erase me,
Worldly friends will ignore me,
But I will not budge.

Worldly strength will fail me,

Worldly knowledge forsakes me,

Worldly actions convict me,

But I will not budge.

No I will not budge.

Though my vision may fail me.

No I will not nudge.

Though my muscles may ail me.

Worldly pressures may crush me,

Worldly winds may rush me,

Worldly death may touch me,

But I will not budge.

For my Father Provides,

And He Is Greater than lies,

In Him we always survive,

Therefore, I Will..Not..Budge.

P6. "Born In War: Poems of Peace"

Poems of Strength/ J. Ellison

I. Poem VI//

The Weight of Battle

Casually we walk through fierce tornados,
Becoming stronger with each step taken.

Blindly we stride into a hurricane,
Empowered amongst each gust of wind shaken.

Bravely we proceed through those turbulent waters,
Becoming wiser into the storm.

Fiercely we stroll through a wall of fire,
Becoming more aware towards flames of harm.

Yes, our fight is of the spirit,
He Grants us rest throughout the battle.

We are grown stronger as we progress,
His Light makes all the evil scatter.

Though the world may come against us,
In Him, we stand secure.

For we are treasured in His Sight,
His Might makes things of man obscure.

Understand, we will not be stopped,
Yes, this is by His Grand Design.

In truth, my Father is GOD of all,
In Him, we never fall behind.

P7. "Born In War: Poems of Peace"

Poems of Strength/ J. Ellison

I. Poem VII//

Not Sinless But Sin Less

We may not be wise, but wiser.

We may not be strong, but stronger.

We may not be better, but better positioned,

Though we may not be, we are as we are.

We may not be of the world, though of the world.

We may not be of it's ways, though born into it's ways.

We may not be viewed as most, though viewed the most.

Though we may not be, we are as we were meant to be.

We may not be lost, but yet are found.

We may not be freed, but yet have hope.

We may not be risen, but yet have Life,

Though we may not be, we are as we shall be.

For the Lord has comforted us in our trials,

Surely, He has made us into varied treasures before Him.

In that we shall forever worship His Glorious ways,

Though we may not currently be, we are exactly as He
Meant us to be.

P8. "Born In War: Poems of Peace"

Poems of Strength/ J. Ellison

I. Poem VIII//

The Hardest Place

The most difficult thing, one can learn to do,
Is lifting up another, though you suffer too.
Though our backs may ache, and our spines may fold,
We endure pain, so that all may grow.

We walk through fire, we walk through cold,
We love in hurt, to clear your road.
So that you may see, so that you may know,
We give our lives, just to save your souls.

For all to see, and for all behold,
Remember His Love, for He Suffered most.
We follow the Lord, for He Makes us whole,
Persist fiercer in Christ, it's in Him we boast.

P9. "Born In War: Poems of Peace"

Poems of Strength/ J. Ellison

I. Poem IX//

We Challenge Us

Break me down to my lowest point,
Build me up to my finest, o brother,
Lord, create in us our true potential,

Through You we challenge each other.

We grow stronger through each trial,
We praise you Father in challenges given,
Refine our measures to become truly greater in Christ,

Through You we challenge in Spirit.

You give the world to be our training ground,
You allow us to overcome fear,
You allow us to be as those mighty in spirit.

Through You we challenge the spear.

You challenge us through the dark times,
You challenge us though we fuss,
You challenge us to challenge each other,

Therefore, we learn to challenge us.

P10. "Born In War: Poems of Peace"

Poems of Strength/ J. Ellison

I. Poem X//

The Strength of a Step

A small key can unlock the greatest treasures.
A small rudder can guide a ship.
The world can change from the smallest measures,
All this in the power of a step.

A beach is made by the smallest sands.
A great split from the smallest rip.
A large battle can be fought from the smallest plan,
Imagine the power in a step.

A huge tree is shaken by the smallest breeze.
A great spear is lead by it's tip.
Even the smallest cloud remains out of reach,
Imagine the force in a step.

Great is one small advance into greatness.

One dream attained is one kept.

GOD is never subject to lateness,

So imagine the dreams through a step.

II. POEMS OF ENDURANCE

P11. "Born In War: Poems of Peace"

Poems of Endurance/ J. Ellison

II. Poem I//

Just Cause

Just Cause I am able to Love, I will.

Just Cause I can reach the finish line, I attempt.

Just Cause someone told me I couldn't do that, I accomplish.

Just Cause you decide to wrong me, doesn't mean I must wrong you.

Just Cause even sitting on the highest hill, is better when you have someone in which to share the view.

Just Cause times are hard, I persist to work even harder.

Just Cause I am able to laugh, I will smile knowing it inspires others.

Just Cause I one day move on from this life, I will be sure build.

Just Cause you say things to hurt me, I will choose to say things instead that heal.

Just Cause my just cause is of the Father, and He Truly

Loves Us All.

I choose to take action Just Cause, My Just Cause Calls.

P12. "Born In War: Poems of Peace"

Poems of Endurance/ J. Ellison

II. Poem II//

A Dream of Weathering Storms

There's a crack in the floor,

In it a dream out of reach.

There's a hole in the wall,

Through it I can see fields of green.

There's a light in the ceiling,

In it I can see darkness flee.

But how long must this last,

This trial brewing in me.

Oh how sweet it must be,

To be that crack in the floor.

For it is always near my dream,

That I couldn't want more.

Oh how fun it would be,
To become the hole in the wall.
For it always can view the beauty,
Of pastures forevermore.

Oh how lovely indeed,
To know the Light overseeing.
For no darkness can be found,
In its presence or gleam.

In time that crack in the floor,
Became a hole in the ground.
While the hole in the wall,
Became a window abound.

Still the light in the ceiling,
Became my way to move on.
Oh how sweet it must be,
To learn to weather the storm.

P13. "Born In War: Poems of Peace"

Poems of Endurance/ J. Ellison

II. Poem III//

Conquered

Though you feel one way,

I say you must do the other.

Though you see evil daily,

I say you will not falter.

Though you move in the world,

I say you will live apart.

Though you want to seek trouble,

I say you will not take part.

Though you constantly battle with me,

I say the victory is won.

Though you want to give up,

I tell you whether the storm.

Though you sometimes get sick,

I say you will not give in.

Though you seek to be lazy,

I tell you be active again.

Though you try to get tired,

I push you on even still.

Because I know that your my body,

You defy me at will.

However, GOD has taken over,

And your conquered in Him.

So toughen up, the war is over,

Body, you're given to Him.

P14. "Born In War: Poems of Peace"

Poems of Endurance/ J. Ellison

II. Poem IV//

I'lol Be Nothing Without You

You tell me I'll be nothing,

Without you starts the suffering.

You tell me the world rejects me,

Without you in the mainstream.

You tell me all lies, all the time,

Just to test me, lol,

You say you're all wise, again lies.

You tell me I'll be something,

If I submit, to your sin.

You tell me I'll be rich when,

I serve you and your mission.

You tell me all lies, all the time,

Just to test me, lol,

My Father sits in Heaven,

He Protects Me.

He conquers you immensely.

His Voice destroys your army.

All you can do is envy,

The Father, Son, who shields me.

Begone! You only tell lies,

Just to test me, lol,

My Father sits in Heaven,

He Protects Me.

P15. "Born In War: Poems of Peace"

Poems of Endurance/ J. Ellison

II. Poem V//

Into The Storm

I wake up only to realize the world is still sleep around me.

I walk daily only to realize people are falling while running upright.

I agonize over their redemption, only to realize they do not agonize over their lives themselves.

I speak knowing that I will be held to a higher standard, because I speak knowing the real Truth.

I debate with love to win over others, though I sometimes lose the their hearts in the end.

I hurt inside when I can't reach them, though I realize their destruction is close.

I love my enemies through the thick of the storm,

Because I know the dangers of corruption.

But still I realize that I must persevere on, because He Gives me that instruction.

P16. "Born In War: Poems of Peace"

Poems of Endurance/ J. Ellison

II. Poem VI//

My Temple from the Lord

My Temple is of the Lord,
Though the world says it's not.

My Faith is what continually drives me,
Though society beckons me to stop.

My Mind is of the Spirit,
Though my thoughts stay in constant battle.

My Voice gives praise to Him,
Though it is constantly fighting negative chatter.

My Presence is from the Lord,
Though I am criticized daily for my stance.

My Heart breathes true love,

Though the world seemingly hates it's advance.

My Feet constantly move forward,

Though the ground under, comes to fade away.

This Temple is called the Holy Body,

Our Church in the Spirit, as we Pray.

My Temple is uniquely powerful,

Designed to conquer by the day.

My Temple is built of the Mighty Lord,

And it is always this way, that it shall ever be set to stay.

P17. "Born In War: Poems of Peace"

Poems of Endurance/ J. Ellison

II. Poem VII//

So Fly Little Bird, Fly

Though a person has no legs, does not mean that person cannot stand.

So run little bird, run.

Though a person has no sight, doesn't mean that person cannot see.

So visualize little bird, visualize.

Though a person has stopped growing physically, doesn't mean that person has stopped growing.

So grow strong little bird, grow strong.

Though a person won't smile, doesn't mean that person can't laugh.

So sing little bird, sing.

Though one has worldly wisdom, it doesn't mean they

always make the best decisions.

So be wise little bird, be wise.

Why?

People mistakenly assume that just because something is seen in one place on a constant basis,

That it should constantly remain there on a constant basis.

Little bird,

Just because it is an understood truth to one,

Doesn't mean it is a universal truth to all.

So go fly little bird, fly.

P18. "Born In War: Poems of Peace"

Poems of Endurance/ J. Ellison

II. Poem VIII//

Born Into A Thunderstorm

Though I was born into a thunderstorm,
Raised through its roar,
Taught to withstand it's rain,
Still I have love.

Though I was thrust into a hurricane,
Raised through its power,
Taught to withstand its devastation,
Still I have love.

Though I was caught up into a tornado,
Raised in its winds,
Taught to endure its full strength,
Still I have love.

Above all things,

Beyond all rains,

Throughout all pain,

Still I have love.

Though I was born into chaos,

Raised in a fallen world,

Taught to survive alone,

Still I have love.

Though I was born into battle,

Raised in the thick of war,

Taught to overcome the pain,

Still I have love.

Though I was born bare in the winter,

Raised in its icy grips,

Taught to endure the freeze,

Still I have love.

For He is the True Sovereign King,

Who Strengthens me,

So above all things,

Still I have love.

P19. "Born In War: Poems of Peace"

Poems of Endurance/ J. Ellison

II. Poem IX//

GOD Is On Your Side

So many things beckon for our attention,
They remove our minds from our goals.
But keep your eyes onto the future,
GOD can handle the workload.

So many ways to become distracted,
One step leads to many paths.
But keep your eyes upon the treasure,
Let the Lord Handle all the maps.

The road ahead seems to become faded,
The journey overwhelms those faint of heart.
But keep your eyes upon finish line,
The Father Carried you from the start.

Though constant problems seem to grow,
Your false friends now begin to show.
But keep your eyes upon the goal,
For He is sustaining through the cold.

So many pains within my heart,
Feeling so drained in every part.
But keep your eyes upon the picture,
For you are His Honored work of art.

So many excuses we tell ourselves,
Too many distractions to ask for help.
But keep those eyes upon the skies,
My Child, GOD Is On Your Side.

P20. "Born In War: Poems of Peace"

Poems of Endurance/ J. Ellison

II. Poem X//

It Starts In You

The smallest flicker could ignite the largest fire.

The faintest breeze could be the harbinger to the most ferocious storm.

The skinniest root can grow into the widest tree.

The tiniest second could one day span into an century.

The lowest glimmer of faith can one day grow into the brightest flare of hope.

The slightest whim of courage could evolve into the fiercest of revolutions.

The one small dream could grow into the very thing that changes the world.

Even the smallest burst of energy could lead to the most powerful explosion the world has ever seen.

It is for this reason that we must each continue in the path He has set for us, though we know not where it takes us.

For through our tiny faith steps, the pathway of peace is created for those to follow after us.

Always, always believe in yourself.

III. POEMS OF EMPOWERMENT

P21. "Born In War: Poems of Peace"

Poems of Empowerment/ J. Ellison

III. Poem I//

Children of Difference

It isn't so bad being different, Children of GOD.

Being different is what makes you stand apart from the darkness.

In truth, each of you were born of the Light,

That Light which reveals the hidden path, few are able to see.

Children of Difference, whom you are,

Don't become afraid to embrace your true nature,

No matter how strange that true nature may seem in light of others.

Children of Difference, which you are,

You were designed to move mountains.

You were designed to become unstoppable.

You were designed to be free.

You are as magnificent as the blazing stars throughout the endless skies,

Though they know not where they fly to in the void of endless space,

They fly nonetheless,

Children of Difference, you were carefully crafted to sail the winds, utilizing the Sovereign breeze of the Most High.

Amen I tell you, you are created differently for a reason My Child.

And it is that difference..which makes you a truly a beautiful sight in the eyes of GOD.

P22. "Born In War: Poems of Peace"

Poems of Empowerment/ J. Ellison

III. Poem II//

Even Still There's Hope

Open your mind to closed minds of those in the world around you.

Train your heart to love, though you may not receive that same love in return.

Strengthen your body through every weakness encountered.

Learn to unlearn any negative habits.

Become empowered by understanding you are not empowered to understand everything.

Understand that though you see before you darkness,

You are of the Light.

Realize that though your surroundings are calm,

You are in the center of a very fierce fight.

Develop yourself to, in turn, develop others.

Remove yourself to help include yourself.

Know that not everything is about you, yet everything is about you.

Even still there's Hope, when we're shown despair.

Even still we see, though we are not taught to stare.

We are born to love, though some refuse to care.

We are children of GOD, those whom He Always Repairs.

P23. "Born In War: Poems of Peace"

Poems of Empowerment/ J. Ellison

III. Poem III//

Only Then Will You Realize

Prepare to grow.
Confront the wall in your path.
Only then will you realize,
That same wall before you,
Becomes smaller in height,
In the face of your continual growth.

Remain determined.
Face the great hill before you.
Only then will you realize,
That same great hill,
Somehow starts to become lesser,
As you strive to continually climb above all obstacles.

Challenge opinion.

Learn to face the world square on,

Only then will you realize,

It will continue to spin regardless,

of other people's thoughts concerning you.

Battle your fear.

Only then will you realize,

Your true Strength lies in GOD,

Who Empowers you to one day realize,

That only then,

Can you truly one day realize.

P24. "Born In War: Poems of Peace"

Poems of Empowerment/ J. Ellison

III. Poem IV//

Unbroken Faith

We learn to live regardless,

Though we do not have life forever.

We actively seek to love others,

Though we do not all come together.

We hold fast the memories of loved ones,

Though they may be slow to remember.

We still wish the best to our enemies,

Though they may treat us still cold as winter.

We seek to see the unseen,

Though true faith is revealed not only by sight.

We enter the battle as the underdog,

Though we know, we win the fight.

We move to empower others,

Though those others may choose not to believe.

We serve the Lord the regardless,

Because through Him we each achieve.

P25. "Born In War: Poems of Peace"

Poems of Empowerment/ J. Ellison

III. Poem V//

Hear Little Dreamer

Hear His Words little dreamer,
Find the knowledge unseen.

There are journeys to be made,
There are visions to seize.

Hear His Voice little dreamer,
Find in His Path through the weeds.

There are treasures to be found,
There are blessings to raise.

Hear His Thoughts little dreamer,
Find His Will to succeed.

There are seas to be sailed,
There are mountains to reach.

Hear His Song little dreamer,
Find His Tune in the breeze.

There are rhythms to be heard,
There is laughter to seek.

Through the sounds of the world,
You can hear it's true beat.
Through the motions of the sea,
You can hear it's heart speak.

Through the laughter of a child,
You can hear the Lord teach.

So hear His Heart little dreamer,
And continue in peace.

P26. "Born In War: Poems of Peace"

Poems of Empowerment/ J. Ellison

III. Poem VI//

Born Again, Again

Once you knew the Lord,
Once you walked in His ways,

But then you became filled,
Your walk became swayed.

You settled for the lesser,
Returned to lost ways.

You walked without GOD,
You turned away Grace.

But you forgot our GOD is greater,
He found you in your stray.

He readjusted your stride,
Then rebuilt you up in place.

He brought you back to His Love,
He helped you turn the page.

He extinguished the flames within,
He helped you calm the rage.

So that again you stand redeemed,
Even from your sinful ways.
For no evil can overcome you,
When the Lord is on the case.

How far you come in struggle,
How fast you have come to race.
All things are now made possible,
For the Lord has set your pace.

P27. "Born In War: Poems of Peace"

Poems of Empowerment/ J. Ellison

III. Poem VII//

It's Too Soon To Quit

Though no one may support my dreams,
Though no one may come to help my needs,
Don't know what ball, father-time may pitch,
But until fate hits, it's too soon to quit.

Though no one may lend me a hand,
Though no one may help me take a stand,
Don't know what ball, father-time may pitch,
But until fate hits, it's too soon to quit.

Though no one may know our true potential,
Though no one may call us influential,
Don't know what ball, father-time may pitch,
But until fate hits, it's too soon to quit.

Though no one may share my heavy burden,
Though no one may know my walk for certain,
Don't know what ball, father-time may pitch,
But until fate hits, it's too soon to quit.

It's too soon to quit, yes too soon to quit,
Though it may be late, it's too soon to quit.

Though no one may give me food when hungry,
Though no one may sit with me when lonely,
Don't know what ball, father-time may pitch,
But until fate hits, it's too soon to quit.

Though no one may understand the way,
Though no one may soon believe the faith,
Don't know what ball, father-time may pitch,
But until fate hits, it's too soon to quit.

P28. "Born In War: Poems of Peace"

Poems of Empowerment/ J. Ellison

III. Poem VIII//

The Gold Prospector

Some dig and dig, then dig some more,

Only to give up before, the hole's gold has been bore.

Others work and work, and work galore,

Just to quit before, the promotion waiting in store.

Some travel and travel, go and travel some more,

But somehow leave before, the cities fully explored.

Others struggle and struggle, just to struggle some more,

Then complain and lose in faith, before the promise restores.

Some train and train, wake and train some more,

Just to give up on their goal, while only inches from score.

Remember why you started, push your will to the core.

You are closer then you were, or were ever before.

You are empowered by the Father, whom He surely adores,

Now find your path, follow His Staff, and continue some more.

P29. "Born In War: Poems of Peace"

Poems of Empowerment/ J. Ellison

III. Poem IX//

Sustaining Grace

Through every argument against me, I stand,
In every conflict, I am protected,
You are my sustainer,
Given to my by the One Who Sustains.

Through every trial upon me, I endure,
In every verdict, I am reassured,
You are my direction,
Planted upon me by the One Who Directs.

Through every difficulty given me, I prosper,
In every tribulation, I am given rest,
You are my redeemer,
Installed unto me by Him Who Redeems.

Through every insult upon me, I forgive,

In every disagreement, I am calmed,

You are my serenity,

Given to me by the One Who Grants Salvation,

Dear Grace of GOD,

We are all covered in His Holy Love for sake of you.

He has given you to alleviate our condemnation.

He has championed us in Christ by way of you.

Dearest Grace of GOD,

You flow upon us throughout all obstacles,

You walk with us throughout all time,

You sit with us while in despair,

Dearest Holy Grace, you comfort us.

P30. "Born In War: Poems of Peace"

Poems of Empowerment/ J. Ellison

III. Poem X//

Fear-Less

There I stand, high on the cliff of impossibility,
There I wonder, about the infinite probabilities,
There I hope, as I gaze into the endless sky,
The wind softly grazing my face, as I watch the seagulls fly.

There I remember, every undiscovered possibility,
There I remember, the vast scope of the world,
There I remember, there is hope above all,
My hearts sings without a missed beat unto the Lord.

There He Answers, "My Child, How Have You Been?"
I Answer, "Dear Lord, as You Allow. Thank You Father."

As the blue sky beckons me,
As the blue sea glistens,

I once again take flight,

High into those clouds above,

For I am the graceful Dove.

The everlasting symbol of His Holy Love.

IV. POEMS OF KNOWLEDGE

P31. "Born In War: Poems of Peace"

Poems of Knowledge/ J. Ellison

IV. Poem I//

In Testing

Every person's morals will be tested in life.

However, it is how that person responds to that test of morals, that determines the actuality of their true morals.

Many are lost though they are of perfect sight,

Many have fallen though they seemingly stand upright,

Pride, lust, and deception, all these things come before the fall,

Honor, Love, Grace, all these things lift the Lord,

Brothers and Sisters remember this,

For it shall serve you well,

You simply cannot serve GOD and money.

P32. "Born In War: Poems of Peace"

Poems of Knowledge/ J. Ellison

IV. Poem II//

The Perspective Change

Some see a glass half full,

I see a glass half empty.

Some see the troubles in the world,

I see the blessings hidden within those troubles.

Some see abandonment as a lifelong burden,

I see it as an opportunity to become stronger.

Some see that some cannot see,

I see that though they cannot see, they can yet still hear.

Some choose to avoid those with contrasting opinions,

I chose to face them head on, and in the process, learn my opinion's defense better.

Some choose to stay grounded, because it seems to be the safest route in life.

I choose to fly freely, because I have known true Life.

Some look to me and turn their nose,

I look to them and hope them growth.

Some may try to destroy all the things I believe,

But I say, just let them be, because He has already destroyed all who come against me,

For some see the Lord clearly, to some degree,

But I see the Lord wholly, from a perspective most fail to see.

For My Lord is GOD of all, can you plant the seed?

Or instead, become the tree from which the good seed repeats.

P33. "Born In War: Poems of Peace"

Poems of Knowledge/ J. Ellison

IV. Poem III//

The Path of Learning

The path we each carve for ourselves in life,

Will determine the burden of our footsteps.

Those footsteps will become our lasting legacy.

That legacy will be passed down to our descendants.

Our descendants will carry on that legacy, through their memories of us.

Those same memories will be returned to GOD, once our lives are gone.

Our GOD will hand those memories over to eternity.

So you see my brothers and sisters,

All that is us becomes eternity inside the Father, For He is True Life.

We were meant to learn from the paths in which we carve in life,

As we were meant to be eternal in Christ.

My dear friends, choose to engage the path which leads eternally towards seeking Christ.

P34. "Born In War: Poems of Peace"

Poems of Knowledge/ J. Ellison

IV. Poem IV//

But I Have Christ

Some people have dreams of more dreams.
Some people have hope in what they've stored.
Some people have goals saturated in success,
But I Have Christ.

Some people have everything on the horizon.
Some people have the entire beach.
Some people don't have to have not,
But I Have Christ.

Some people may frown on me.
Some people may reject my spoken words.
Some people may grow to war against me,
But I Have Christ.

For those people have temporary treasures,

For all this world to behold.

But He Has treasure eternal,

His Word is better than gold.

P35. "Born In War: Poems of Peace"

Poems of Knowledge/ J. Ellison

IV. Poem V//

Interconnected Through Uncertainty

Just as the air becomes one with the vastness of the sky,

So must we all become one in the ways of the Holy Lord.

Just as the wise owl knows his place around the tree, but does not understand the grand plan of the forest,

So must we each seek to understand our place granted us, though we do not understand His Grand design for us.

Just as a meal is consumed as a portion throughout the day, so that the body can properly digest it,

So must we also consume the portions of knowledge granted us, so that we do not become overwhelmed by that knowledge granted us.

Just as the water runs the course of the entire river, interval by interval, to one day reach the oceanfront.

So must we proceed throughout each day, moment by moment, to one day reach our coveted goals.

Does not the bird fly regardless of knowing where it is to take flight?

Does the bird say, "Because I can see no end, there is no point in me flying high?"

Does not the wind continue blow, though it may not be clearly known where it originates?

Does not it continue in its task to provide its gentle breeze to the world nonetheless?

My friends, follow His Will regardless of where it leads you.

For where you end up according to His Holy Will is exactly where you are to be and were meant to be.

Look not with your eyes, but through His Eyes granted you.

There you will find, that you have been found all along.

P36. "Born In War: Poems of Peace"

Poems of Knowledge/ J. Ellison

IV. Poem VI//

The Wisdom in Clouds

The clouds stare down,
Gazing on humanity.

The clouds see all,
Floating in serenity.

The clouds bear witness,
For they were created from infinity.

The clouds watched man,
Since they were spoken from Divinity.

The Lord made clouds,
To cloak the sky in amenities.

The clouds fly high,

They need no permission or validity.

The clouds promote change,

They bare the rain for fertility.

The clouds are of Heaven,

Bringing our thoughts to visibility.

Imagine the secrets,

The clouds have hidden in their melody.

The clouds were bore wise,

They ride the wind in stability.

Learn from the clouds,

For they adapt in their ability.

Remember the cloud,

When you measure versatility.

P37. "Born In War: Poems of Peace"

Poems of Knowledge/ J. Ellison

IV. Poem VII//

Water Unto The Spirit

Just as the physical body cannot be without water,

So the spiritual body cannot be without the Holy Spirit.

Just as water comes in many forms,

So does the Holy Spirit also come in many forms.

Just as water cleanses all regardless of stain,

So does the Holy Spirit also work to cleanse all without prejudice.

Just as water flows freely from its true source on earth,

So does the Holy Spirit flow freely from His true source in Heaven.

Just as water serves to strengthen a person's weakened state,

So does the Holy Spirit also serve to strengthen a person's weakened state.

Water refreshes the spirit,

Just as the Holy Spirit becomes the water of the spirit.

Water is freely given to man from the sky, just as the Holy Spirit is freely given from the sky to man.

The Holy Spirit is of GOD, just as water is of GOD's creation.

Understand for this reason, water is used to baptize all in the ways of Jesus Christ, so that they may receive the Holy Spirit.

For we are all to become eternally holy once reborn in Christ,

However, the Holy Spirit remains forever the living water of Jesus Christ.

When you speak of the Holy Spirit, remember the lesson given to you by GOD's water.

However, the next time you drink water, remember the true lesson given to you by GOD's Holy Spirit residing within us all.

P38. "Born In War: Poems of Peace"

Poems of Knowledge/ J. Ellison

IV. Poem VIII//

Age and Time

Just as a fresh flower is in full bloom until the time of the season changes,

So does the youthful human body grow to mature into time.

Just as wine becomes better with time,

So does one also become wiser over the course of age.

There is a hidden beauty in age,

Just as there is revealed beauty in time.

For one's true beauty is revealed through age.

Just as one's true understanding is revealed through time.

Time reveals age, as age reveals time.

Though age and time walk hand in hand,
I tell you, wisdom is born of this dance.

For some may hide and some may show,
One's age begets wisdom,
That time will bestow.

But hear me well, be wise to know,
Time is a teacher, the Father controls.

Though time may pass, and age may grow,
Remember the Lord, and your strength shall flow.

P39. "Born In War: Poems of Peace"

Poems of Knowledge/ J. Ellison

IV. Poem IX//

The Disciplined Disciple

Though a protruding nail become hammered down through a board,

It does not complain about the blow,

For it serves to attach the wood regarding the project at hand.

Though an ant may alone carry a large load on it's back to it's nest,

It does not complain about the weight given it,

For it works to build up the colony to better preserve it's future.

Though a tree bear a heavy load within it's branches,

It does not complain about their length and height,

For it's branches are what bears it's sweet fruit, in order to spread it's future seeds.

Though the ocean continually ripples,

It does not complain about the movements given it,

For it's motions of current are what helps to balance the life of all the wildlife within it.

Though the heart beats heavily non-stop, day in and day out,

It does not complain about the workload given,

For it serves to regulate the blood flow of the entire body in which it operates.

My point is this dear disciple,

Though we become disciplined or given a great workload from the Lord, do not complain,

For every great difficulty we face, is meant to refine us for the overall greater good,

Thus, making us greater leaders in the sight of the Lord.

Lovely disciple,

Never lose heart when the Lord disciplines you.

For He Disciplines all those He Loves and has truly accepted as a son.

Become grateful instead.

P40. "Born In War: Poems of Peace"

Poems of Knowledge/ J. Ellison

IV. Poem X//

Rhymes In Rhymes

This simply happens to happen to those who happen to have happenings happening,

All the time, in time, but time can time, and time again,

Test with tests, of tests to test, and test, one's test of tests,

For minds, of minds, but mind, that minds will mind,

Those trials of trials, in trial, though trials may trial, their trials of trials,

With signs of signs, a sign, can sign one's sign, to sign,

But await in wait, for wait, can wait, when wait, can wait,

Through rhymes of rhymes, when rhymes, can rhyme, for rhymes to rhyme,

Defined:

This simply happens, all the time,

Test with tests, for minds of minds.

Trials of trials, with signs of signs,

Await in wait, through rhymes of rhymes.

V. POEMS OF LOVE

P41. "Born In War: Poems of Peace"

Poems of Love/ J. Ellison

V. Poem I//

Since Forever

I've Loved You,

From the time you opened your eyes,

Through the time you took your first steps,

Into the time your diaper was first changed,

Ever since the time you begin to first dream,

From the time you were hurt from falling as you played,

To the time you entered first high school,

Through the time you first had your heart broken,

Into the time you finally graduated college,

From the time you first matured and became married,

Through the time you began your own family,

From the time you grew older and massively wiser,

Throughout the time you were first diagnosed,

Into the time you were placed into an elderly nursing home for additional care,

Until the time you smiled and gave your last breath,

My Child, I've loved you through eternity,

Through the time before time itself was established,

Through before the universe was ever conceived,

I've Loved You Since Forever Dear Child..

And I shall Continue to Love You Far Far Beyond That.

P42. "Born In War: Poems of Peace"

Poems of Love/ J. Ellison

V. Poem II//

A Soulmate's Song

Without your touch I feel incapable of breathing,

Without your laughter there is no pain worth healing,

Without your Words the sky doesn't seem so blue,

Without you I am not myself,

Without you, there is simply no me without you.

Without you the busy world seems to come to a screeching pause,

Without you long walks become a day of daydream without meaning,

Without you my love seems to be without love itself,

For you are my soulmate, in whom GOD so beautifully blessed me with,

My cool shadow in the heat of a blazing sun,

My cool breeze in the midst of a beautiful summer storm,

My constant beat deep within my Heart,

My constant trust even when all else falls apart.

You are my true soulmate, whom the Lord has made for me in His Everlasting Love,

You are His Direct Proof that nothing in this World can describe His True Love!

P43. "Born In War: Poems of Peace"

Poems of Love/ J. Ellison

V. Poem III//

Inseparable: Wife

My world spins within your world.

My heart humbly gives it's beat to yours.

My feet walk the unknown path, that together we have come to create.

My legacy is your legacy.

My anything surrenders to your everything,

Your everything beckons me to accomplish anything.

You are my relaxation from a busy day.

You are my best friend given to me by My Best Friend in Heaven.

In my eyes, you are the best thing to ever be, the gift of perfection perfected.

You are like the warmth that a sweet smile brings in a cool summer rain.

Along with the Father, your quenching conversation is the constant refreshment I thirst for daily.

He designed you to complete the puzzle to the picture

which is called my life.

For He loved us so, that He created our love to reach new uncharted Holy heights.

By Way of the Most High, I promise to always love and defend,

My truly talented and very precious Wife,

Whom GOD has created masterfully,

To walk together with me for Life.

P44. "Born In War: Poems of Peace"

Poems of Love/ J. Ellison

V. Poem IV//

Even Still He Loves You

Though you make fun of Him,
Still He Loves You.

Though you falter in your walk,
Still He Loves You.

Though you temporarily fall in the battle with sin,
Still He Loves You.

Though you realize how wrong you were in that moment,
Still He Loves You.

Though your loved ones may turn their backs on you,
Still He Loves You.

Though your heart has been broken over and over again,

Still He Loves You.

Though those you truly loved have passed away at some point in life,

Still He Loves You.

Though you look down on those who continue to follow Him,

Still He Loves You.

Though governments may remove Him from your schools and society,

Still He Loves You.

Though the entire world may come to one day doubt Him,

Still He Loves You.

There is nothing in or out of existence that can separate His Eternal Love from you.

Though the world may end. Though time may cease. My Child, you must always remember this,

Even Still He Loves You.

P45. "Born In War: Poems of Peace"

Poems of Love/ J. Ellison

V. Poem V//

Only Time Will Tell

Where we go from here,
We grow to go together.
Where we dream from here,
Only time will tell.

Where we fly from here,
Our spirits soar together.
Where we begin that flight,
Only time will tell.

Where we ride the wind,
We hit the skies together.
Where that breeze may take us,
Only time will tell.

Where we walk and stumble,
We stop the fall together.
Where the ground should move,
Only time will tell.

Where you love, I love,
We stop the world together.
Where every second may go,
Only time will tell.

For every moment we share,
Creates a memory together.
How that bond lives on,
Only time will tell.

My life takes joy in your smile,
He Makes us partners forever.
Where the Father May Guide us,
Only time will tell.

When Heaven should one day call,

We'll take the phone together.

For my heart is your heart,

Our love endures forever.

P46. "Born In War: Poems of Peace"

Poems of Love/ J. Ellison

V. Poem VI//

Until You Were Born

I seemed to be alone in life,
Until the day you were born.

I suffered many breakups,
Was heartbroken many times,
But still I didn't learn true love,
Until the day you were born.

I walked in worldly ways,
Fought every battle in vain,
But didn't truly walk straight,
Until the day you were born.

I conquered every mountain,
Journeyed through every valley,

But knew not my finest triumph,

Until the day you were born.

I moved through the darkest waters,

Flew through the violent winds,

Pushed through the hottest deserts,

Until the day you were born.

For when GOD allowed me to find you,

I knew then my true purpose.

Dear Marriage,

Your birth is has made everything worth it.

P47. "Born In War: Poems of Peace"

Poems of Love/ J. Ellison

V. Poem VII//

The Sunset's Song

Your smile lights up the world.

Your smile makes all whom see you appear to be of sweet golden light.

Your calmness decimates the exhausting heat of the day.

Your unwanted absence is always followed by darkness.

Nevertheless you dramatically appear everyday in your magnificent beauty.

You are a beautiful painting to behold against that canvas which is the sky.

You are an swift surprising treasure to behold each day against the eternal grace of Heaven.

My Lord has crafted and created you into many masterpieces.

For you know His Heart, and He Opts to speak to us directly through you daily.

In you everything is made as a beautiful creation.

For you are the very gracious sunset given to us in love's manifestation.

A true sight handed to us from the Holy Father above.

One of many many symbols given to us everyday to firmly declare the power in His Eternal Holy Love.

P48. "Born In War: Poems of Peace"

Poems of Love/ J. Ellison

V. Poem VIII//

For Your Smile

Cause I'd rather see You Smile,
Before I adjust style,
Or worry in these trials.
I'd rather know Your Smile,
Then walk in any lies,
Or proceed empty miles.

I'd rather walk the thousands miles,
Barefoot through the thorns,
Just to reconcile.
I'd rather endure every trial,
Face the pain,
Just to gain,
You the Paramount.

I'd rather swim a thousand miles,
With broken arms in a storm,
Just to seek You out.
I'd rather live a thousand lives,
Then give up You,
Or Your Ways,
For a large amount.

I'd rather fight a thousand lies,
From every mouth in a crowd,
Just to clear the clouds.
I'd rather clear out all denial,
From every lip set against You,
To remove the doubt.

I'd rather give You everything,
Every joy ever thought,
Just to sing You Praise.
I'd rather serve You everyday,
To one day see Your Face,
And pass into Your Grace.

Cause I'd rather see You Smile,

Before I adjust style,

Or worry in these trials.

I'd rather know Your Smile,

Then walk in any lies,

Or proceed empty miles.

P49. "Born In War: Poems of Peace"

Poems of Love/ J. Ellison

V. Poem IX//

Regardless He Loves

The Lord Will Love you regardless,

Doesn't matter what you make.

The Lord Will Love you regardless,

You don't need to buy His Grace.

The Lord Will Love you regardless,

Nevermind your social status.

The Lord Will Love you regardless,

He doesn't care about your credit.

The Lord Is with you regardless,

It doesn't matter what they say.

The Lord Is with you regardless,
In every moment of the day.

The Lord Is with you regardless,
As you seek to ever pray.

The Lord Is with you regardless,
Though most criticize your faith.

Regardless He Loves regardless,
Though most think He Is Heartless.
Regardless He Loves regardless,
Though some seek Him in bargain.

Regardless He Loves regardless,
Those some slander to market.
Regardless He Loves regardless,
But He Always on target.

P50. "Born In War: Poems of Peace"

Poems of Love/ J. Ellison

V. Poem X//

Faith Is Love

Though I wake up everyday,
In a new struggle to face.
Though I look up to the sky,
And yet can only see gray,

I still believe, my Lord Relieves.
This faith is love, true air to breathe.

Though some family lose their way,
On their walk into Grace.
Though some battle within race,
Speaking hate as their case.

I still believe, my Lord Relieves.
This faith is love, true air to breathe.

When a loved one, one day strays,
And it causes you aches.
When you feel above of your age,
And it saddens your pace.

Then still believe, our Lord Relieves.
This faith is love, true air to breathe.

When all is lost in your thoughts,
And the end seems vague.
When every path is a toss,
Know the Lord's in place.

We still believe, our Lord Relieves.
This faith is love, true air to breathe.

VI. POEMS OF INSPIRATION

P51. "Born In War: Poems of Peace"

Poems of Inspiration/ J. Ellison

VI. Poem I//

Persistence Born

Before becoming a dreambuilder. I was:

1. Lost as a child.

2. Told by a kindergarten teacher, I would never become anything.

3. Drowned at 12.

4. Exposed to the first hand effects of drugs, as a kid, due to our location.

5. Evicted.

6. Called derogatory names.

7. Saved from a potentially devastating car crash.

8. Without a job. Without a dream.

9. Without many friends.

But still I:

1. Located my lost family.

2. Graduated High School.

3. Got a academic scholarship to college.

4. Enlisted in the military.

5. Served in support of the Special Forces.

6. Jumped out of a plane on multiple occasions.

7. Survived 4x Deployments.

8. Commissioned as an Army Officer.

9. Traveled to Italy, France, England, Switzerland, Greece, Ireland, Germany, Prague, Croatia, UAE, Dubai, Kuwait, Qatar, Jordan, the Netherlands, Iraq, and Afghanistan.

10. Received molding guidance from over 15x Army General Officers.

11. Became a Husband and a father.

12. Became a graphic designer, film director, photographer, author, and a servant of Christ.

My point is this:

How can you say there is no GOD? Surely it is Him who has brought us this far in proving everyone who doubted us wrong. Brothers and Sisters, I tell you don't worry about what we've done in the past. Focus instead on the obstacles He will have us conquer next. We are the Future.

P52. "Born In War: Poems of Peace"

Poems of Inspiration/ J. Ellison

VI. Poem II//

Sweet Redemption

Out of the Ashes, my true life breathes,

From destruction, I become Holy.

Though death has birthed me, I have been given over to Life,

Though my actions have destroyed me, I have become stronger through those experiences.

Even though I was warned before I drowned, I breathe again today through His Resurrection,

Even covered in filth, I have become cleaned.

Though my hardships have conquered me before, I stand now before You triumphant,

Though my dreams were violently snatched away, they are now freely given unto me.

Even when the pain inside struck me to the ground, You
Softly lifted me up to my feet,

Even through the time when my heart seemingly stopped,
You Granted me life forever more.

I am forgiven, and through You I am forever redeemed.

Your servant, child, and creation as I was truly meant to
be.

P53. "Born In War: Poems of Peace"

Poems of Inspiration/ J. Ellison

VI. Poem III//

The Everyday Miracle

You are an everyday miracle,

Uniquely and specifically designed.

You have a specific set of talents,

Which comes from your unique genetic make up.

This specific genetic process has allowed you be created with a unique set of fingerprints,

Allowing you specifically occupy and hold a unique way of life.

You have been given specifically to your parents,

To occupy and fill a unique space within the world.

Specifically, you have been assigned to a unique place in time, at a specific moment, for a unique reason.

You were additionally assigned specific dreams, to achieve using an unique route, specifically designed for you.

You are specifically awesome, and uniquely perfect,

There will never BE another you.

My Father has created an everyday miracle out of you to be specific.

The only unique person qualified to be you, out of the billions specifically placed in the world, is you.

P54. "Born In War: Poems of Peace"

Poems of Inspiration/ J. Ellison

VI. Poem IV//

The Crowd Fades Away

In the heat of this race,

the track is always crowded.

The sounds of those cheering become blurred.

Only the intensity of the competition remains.

The animosity of a dream becoming achieved hangs in the balance.

Speeding thoughts race of never coming in second.

The heart seems to begin beating louder and harder than it ever has ever before.

The excitement builds towards the race which lies ahead.

At this point the mind becomes clear.

The body moves as it has been constantly trained.

The crowded track seems to now become less cluttered.

The path lying ahead seems to be becoming more clear by the moment.

All of the crowds chanting and cheering, fades away in the excitement.

Now focused, we realize there is no one else around us.

As we run towards our goal,
On the track which is life.
Knowing not many will finish,
But we still continue the fight.
We steady race towards our dreams,
Though they are not always in sight.
So rejoice Strong of Heart!
Even in the thick of the fight.
When we are one with the Father,
We become prone to take flight.
For it is He who gives us wings,
In this race we call Life.

P55. "Born In War: Poems of Peace"

Poems of Inspiration/ J. Ellison

VI. Poem V//

Lifted

There is no earthly weight capable of holding us down.

There is no worldly chain to pull us back from the sky towards the ground.

There is no battle set from the enemy which can truly overcome us.

There is no earthly war fought that can truly dethrone us.

There is no taunt capable of removing the Lord's Eternal Love.

There is no wish that can be snatched away from our grasp given from high above.

There is no destruction set to conquer the True Light of this world.

There is nothing more beautiful than you in His Word.

There is nothing between us and the love of Christ.

For what is a mountain before us, when we have GOD guiding our sight.

We are Children of GOD and this shall always be,

We remain lifted in His Love, His Word sets us free.

P56. "Born In War: Poems of Peace"

Poems of Inspiration/ J. Ellison

VI. Poem VI//

Imagine Life

Imagine a perfect world,
In which Heaven oversees.
Imagine a lost thought,
Given life in the breeze.

Imagine a lost child,
Who has never known heartbreak.
Imagine the smile made,
When the Lord becomes his playmate.

Imagine the joy brought,
From a life never destroyed.
Imagine no anger ever,
What a sight to be restored.

Imagine the happiness,

Of a child not aborted.

Imagine a foreign land,

From which you can never be deported.

Imagine your endless dreams,

Flying high through the sky.

Imagine the Lord's Word,

Standing by to provide.

Imagine a vision true,

To the heart of our Christ.

Imagine the battle fought,

Just to grant you True Life.

P57. "Born In War: Poems of Peace"

Poems of Inspiration/ J. Ellison

VI. Poem VII//

iRise

Though my body is sore,

Still I rise.

Though I feel mentally drained,

Still I plan.

Though it is early and I am stubborn to wake up,

Still I open my eyes.

Though I know the day which lies ahead may be difficult,

Still I endure it.

Though the thought of bad news has recently entered my mind,

Still I praise Him.

Though my sight is blurry,
Still I walk.

Though an ailment irritates me,
Still I have hope.

Though the world may give up on me,
I will not give up on it.

Though the sky may one day fall,
And the ground one day give way.
I know the Lord is my Shepard,
I will not lose faith.

In Him, we all become whole,
Though we see turbulent waves.
Those waters will one day lessen,
To reveal the path He Creates.

P58. "Born In War: Poems of Peace"

Poems of Inspiration/ J. Ellison

VI. Poem VIII//

We've Been Thinking Of You

We were thinking of you dear brother,
We've been thinking of you dear sister,
No matter the place or the problems you ensue,
Someone here is praying for you.

How have you held up in the battle?
How have you endured in times for the Truth?
No matter the weight of the issues that you currently face,
Someone is in prayer for you.

O' how the world destroys your true value,
How the world gives way your boot,
For no matter the path that you find yourself on,
Someone here is praying for you.

You will conquer into the valley,

Let every victory stand as the proof,

For no matter the venue that you find yourself in,

Know the Church is praying for you.

In everything, we are constant of thought,

Of everything, you are always in our thoughts,

For no matter the time or the issues that ensue,

Remember we are praying for you,

Dear brother and sister.

P59. "Born In War: Poems of Peace"

Poems of Inspiration/ J. Ellison

VI. Poem IX//

Have You Considered GOD?

Have you considered GOD when:

a.) Your day's been riddled with challenges

b.) Your day's been wrought with bad news

c.) Your hope started to somehow dwindle

d.) Your path forward has given no clue.

Do you consider the Father when:

a.) Your strength has been extracted

b.) Your battle outcome is gloom

c.) Your faith has been retracted

d.) Your life feels like a tomb

Really consider the Father when:

a.) You know you're being tested

b.) You're energy has been consumed

c.) Your demise is soon expected

d.) You're the elephant in the room

Always consider the Father when:

a.) You speak of the resurrected

b.) You walk in Christ renewed

c.) You move in the Holy Spirit

d.) All of the above questions apply to you

P60. "Born In War: Poems of Peace"

Poems of Inspiration/ J. Ellison

VI. Poem X//

For Heaven Will Come

Our time in the world, is short but great,
To learn of His many lessons.

Our hope in GOD transcends all creation,
Our Father Whom Guides our blessings.

For joys of this world are small compared,
To those received of Heaven.

For all are saved, in Christ who paid,
Whom died and rose to reckon,

Our sins erased, our freedom found,
Our life changed in a second.

Receive these words, and hear them well,
Until the day you exit.

We were bore from Heaven, unto the world,
Though its ways have become rejected.

We must inject Christ, into all life,
To cure what sin infected.

Once all is done, and Christ returned,
All evil will become ejected.

For Heaven will come, for the world reborn,
Now established forever protected.

VII. POEMS OF FAITH

P61. "Born In War: Poems of Peace"

Poems of Faith/ J. Ellison

VII. Poem I//

That's Grace

To know you are not worthy, but still acquire His forgiveness.

To understand the only way to truly gain control, is to completely relinquish all control to Him.

To continue living each day to the fullest, knowing very well a grave sickness grows within you.

To give trust, when you feel you've been betrayed, simply because the Father asks.

To help a person some consider to be a lost cause, simply because you can still see hope.

To befriend a person, without a friend, in the moments before they consider ending their life.

To applaud the accomplishments of a not so close friend, though they have not applauded your own.

To establish a foundational hope for those without, though you secretly have not yourself.

These things require faith,

The belief in things unseen though hidden from the beholder's sight.

For without faith we are nothing,

Yet through faith we are made to be everything.

Brothers and Sisters, let your faith guide you. For it is what carves the path to Eternal Life.

P62. "Born In War: Poems of Peace"

Poems of Faith/ J. Ellison

VII. Poem II//

One Day That One Day Comes

One day the parties will end,
It is that day the celebrations will begin,
One day that one day will come.

One day money will be left behind,
It is that day the true treasure will be found,
One day that one day will come.

One day the all sin will be erased,
It is that day all righteousness will continue,
One day that one day will come.

Know that one day the pain will cease,
It's in that day all joy will then consume,
So know one day that one day will come.

One day the path we follow may end,
It is that day that our true journey begins,
So know one day that one day will come.

So that one day those lost may be found,
It is that day that all blind will then see.
So know one day that one day will come.

So that one day that one day comes.

P63. "Born In War: Poems of Peace"

Poems of Faith/ J. Ellison

VII. Poem III//

Thoughts of The Lord

All thoughts of You brighten my everyday.
Your Glory is unfathomable to our understanding.

Your Love Spoke the universe into creation.
Your Knowledge is above all comprehending!

O' how joyous it is to serve You!
How beautiful it is to sing Your Praise!

Before I was known, You Knew me.
It was then I was thought of in Grace.

Before I was given to my family,
It was then I was with You for place.

I am honored to bow before you!

I am honored to utter your name!

For You Are the Glory of all glories!

Every reason of which we each sing praise!

P64. "Born In War: Poems of Peace"

Poems of Faith/ J. Ellison

VII. Poem IV//

Seeing Beyond The Wall

I'm seeing beyond the wall now,

Though no route climb or crawl,

But these chains seem mighty light now, Cause He Reveals the hidden door.

Every argument precedes a bond broken,

Every word uttered, a moment lost,

Every motion gestured destroys momentum,

Every action removes our thoughts.

But I'm seeing beyond the wall now,

Though no route climb or crawl,

But these chains seem mighty light now, Cause He Reveals the hidden door.

No, we can't forget, how far we've come,

The many mountains, we've come to move,

The problems we've known, the tremendous storms,

The pains we've conquered through.

Still I'm seeing beyond the wall now,

Though no route climb or crawl,

But these chains seem mighty light now, Cause He Reveals the hidden door.

How can we forget Who Sustains Us,

The many paths He's Set before,

Becoming as those forgotten His Ways,

Once back to life before.

Yes, I'm seeing beyond the wall now,

Though no route climb or crawl,

But these chains seem mighty light now, Cause He Reveals the hidden door.

I now chose to lose the argument,

So we both may win in the end,

As to not to trick, but though reset,

To not lose sight of Him.

Though, we're seeing beyond the wall now,

Though no route climb or crawl,

But these chains seem mighty light now, Cause He Reveals the hidden door.

Though there is no way of true measure,

Into the size of planted dreams,

We will still believe, we though we disagree,

We grow to plant the seeds.

Yes, we're seeing beyond the wall now,

Though no route climb or crawl,

These chains seem mighty light now, Cause He Reveals the path for all.

P65. "Born In War: Poems of Peace"

Poems of Faith/ J. Ellison

VII. Poem V//

Against All Stares

Like a dreamer against those built in doubt,

Like a builder before those known to destroy,

Like a believer facing a crowd in disbelief,

Face me down, but I persist through all stares.

Like an outsider standing against a foreign land,

Like a righteous man against those who sin,

Like one in a purpose before those without,

Face me down, but I persist through all stares.

Like a rose within a field of weeds,

Like a lone cloud in an empty sky,

Like a lion placed within a den of tigers,

Face me down, but I endure, through all stares.

Against all odds, I stand,

The Lord Has Made me a fortress,

The Lord Has Given me shelter,

The Lord Has Prospered me,

Against all odds, I shall have faith,

Against all odds, I shall fight,

Against all odds, face me down in stance,

For against all odds, I stand,

Face me down,

I endure,

Against all stares.

P66. "Born In War: Poems of Peace"

Poems of Faith/ J. Ellison

VII. Poem VI//

It's GO Time

The race isn't going to run itself.

Standing still doesn't bring the finish line any closer.

To be better tomorrow, you must first learn to conquer today.

In order to attain the goal set before you,

Understand first how to score.

If you want the Lord bad enough, then go after Him.

If you want Him bad enough, but have not yet attained Him,

Then you DO NOT want Him bad enough.

Is not everyday a new day?

Is not every passing second,

A second never before experienced?

Then why stop now,

Christ is your total strength.

All you need is faith to be great.

So what are you waiting for?

Dear Child of GOD.

I say again, what are you waiting for?

Wake up your spirit.

It's GO Time.

P67. "Born In War: Poems of Peace"

Poems of Faith/ J. Ellison

VII. Poem VII//

Because You

Because You Are the Living King.

Because You woke me up without a care,

I worship in the Lord.

Because You. Became.

So that I may be.

Because You Showed in me new dreams,

Because You woke me up in Your Honor,

I worship in the Lord.

Because You. Became.

So that I may be.

Because You Placed me on your team,

Because You Lifted me when no one dared,

We worship in the Lord.

Because You. Became.

So that we may be.

Because You will stomp out all evil,

Because You overcome all adversaries,

We each overflow in grace.

Because You. Became.

So that we each, may continually be.

We worship in the Lord.

P68. "Born In War: Poems of Peace"

Poems of Faith/ J. Ellison

VII. Poem VIII//

Clamors For Attention

Attention attempts for attention,
Your conditions were meant for convincing.
But mentions of things, removed from our brains,
Provokes new aims of prevention.

You clamor for fame by mentioning names,
But really your game is retention.
No matter the frame of your engine,
Or the pitching of better inventions.

You envision a better rendition,
But your mission is better in fiction.
Nevertheless the veteran lesson,
Is a blessing to those who will listen.

And seeing beyond comprehension,
Is His Blessing towards building your pension.
Though you cringe the syringe,
The end can begin, whenever you change composition.

Don't battle for strings of magicians,
Rather settle for dreams in His Vision.
For His Sample is destiny hidden,
And His Mantle is heavenly given.

P69. "Born In War: Poems of Peace"

Poems of Faith/ J. Ellison

VII. Poem IX//

Switching Sides

A losing mindset, cannot make one a winner,

Lest He becomes the winner of losing.

Have faith.

An unfocused mind, cannot overcome a focused one,

Lest that mind becomes the focus of the unfocused one.

Grow strong.

A negative-minded individual cannot bring a positive-minded individual happiness,

Lest that positive-minded individual attain a degree of happiness from helping the negative-minded individual.

Be persistent.

A person can not serve both the ways of good and those of evil.

Lest the ways of darkness in him, become extinguished as he grows towards those ways of the good.

Live Holy.

A person lost in spirit cannot properly comprehend the true ways of the Lord,

Lest through being lost he becomes found towards those ways of the Lord.

Remain Graceful.

A person cannot serve GOD and follow treasure,

Lest the person's treasure resides truly within the Lord.

Become Humble.

See the world from His Perspective.

If you remain negative, you will never see the positive in life.

True change begins within the mind.

True change begins when old ways end.

True change is found only in Christ.

P70. "Born In War: Poems of Peace"

Poems of Faith/ J. Ellison

VII. Poem X//

The End of Battle

Fighting this battle for many years,
My sword his not known rest.

Pushing for hope out of many tears,
My shield is bent from stress.

I must have faith. My every action matters.
For I will endure. Till the end of battle.

Walking this path from the beginning,
My limbs are bruised from trials.

Understanding I'm miles from winning,
And this pace may take awhile.

Still I must have faith. My every action matters.

For I will endure. Till the end of battle.

Every second brings on a new attack,

My mind is weary in anticipation.

Every step reveals a new advance,

My heart beats determination.

Still I must have faith. My every action matters.

For I will endure. Till the end of battle.

Once all pain is vanquished,

Continue to fight in His Glory.

For He Has always taught me patience,

In time, He Will Restore me.

For I must have faith. My every action matters.

Still I will endure. Till the end of battle.

VIII. POEMS OF WISDOM

P71. "Born In War: Poems of Peace"

Poems of Wisdom/ J. Ellison

VIII. Poem I//

Anyhow

Brothers and Sisters realize this,

Not all people like to see you succeed in life..Succeed Anyhow.

Not all may like you for deciding to follow your dreams..Dare to Dream Anyhow.

Not all people will like your facebook post, simply because of who you are..Be Yourself Anyhow.

You cannot find happiness in trying to please others,

You only hurt yourself in the process of seeking their acceptance,

Seek to please the Lord instead. Beautiful child, Don't ever be ashamed to be Yourself.

Continue to show Love to those who doubt you, and when in doubt..Show Love Anyhow.

P72. "Born In War: Poems of Peace"

Poems of Wisdom/ J. Ellison

VIII. Poem II//

Trust Lives

To travel an unseen path, only revealed by the One who designed it.

To build the initial foundation, without fully knowing how the home will turn out.

To work tirelessly day and night, without knowing when and if your time of rest will ever arrive.

To carry a person who may be facing trials in life, though you know not when their time of trial may cease.

To believe in one self, though a immovable mountain lies in squarely your path.

To care for one disabled, knowing not if they will ever grow to have a normal life.

To nurture one injured, though that person may never heal properly.

To battle an grave illness, though another person has already passed away from it, and time seems seemingly short.

To persevere on the playing field of life, though tired and the opposite team seems to be winning.

To continue loving a family member or friend, though they have hurt you continuously, and do not realize it.

To go out on a limb, in reach of a coveted dream, firmly nested on a brittle branch.

All these things, Brothers and Sisters, require Trust. It is that essential Trust, that the true Lord provides for each readily willing to receive it. So rejoice family! You have that beautiful Trust firmly nested within each of you!

P73. "Born In War: Poems of Peace"

Poems of Wisdom/ J. Ellison

VIII. Poem III//

Social Inspiration

When some think of social media, the world seems to be alive.

Some wake up to post a "everything is awesome" status, though they may be hurt or lost inside.

Some manage to tell themselves, if no one hits the "like" button, I'll truly never care.

But in truth, they quietly seek acceptance, for we all have our own burdens to bear.

Some scroll their friends walls in search the day's events, only to find themselves judging others.

Some simply don't make sense, but still they sense the need to make a scene.

Some compare their current lives to those they once knew closely,

But if they are seemingly doing better, without them in their lives, they quietly keep scrolling.

Some sign up to seek acceptance, though that acceptance seldom comes.

Some rush to add a million plus friends,

But in actuality, those some only have one.

Some strive to look good for those online,

But really they are seeking inner validation.

Though without the glamour, underneath the armor, anyone can find the good,

But nevertheless great child, remember this always, you need not seek others to be understood.

For the Father who sees you from Heaven is truly all you need.

Beautiful one, hear these words, don't ever stress about a "like",

Because you living your actual life is dramatically more important than any social media site.

Every second the Father sees your true life status, and He will never continue to scroll.

He Loves you more than anything, and that's truly the greatest story ever told.

P74. "Born In War: Poems of Peace"

Poems of Wisdom/ J. Ellison

VIII. Poem IV//

Learning from Hardships

Before:

I was placed here to teach you important lessons.

I was given to you to assist in molding your ways, inner and external.

I was given to grow you.

I was handed to you to help develop your love for others.

However:

I was not meant to destroy you.

I was not sent to punish you.

I was not always present in your life.

I was not given to you in increments you could not handle.

Instead:

I was placed upon you to make you wiser.

I was cast upon you so that you may follow the correct path.

I was thrust upon you for being to greedy.

I was made a part of your life, because you had not the true Life in Christ.

I was included unto you because you had no direction.

And Then:

I was removed from you because you learned that valuable lesson in some shape or form.

I was taken from you because His Sacrifice demanded it, once you chose to receive it.

I was lifted from you because He Lifts All Burdens.

I was raised from you, because I found no reason more to come upon you.

Because:

I am your "Hardships in Life".

Everything of me that has ever weighed you down, was only meant to one day lift you up towards Christ.

Believe it or not, the Father Loves you massively for bearing me faithfully and fruitfully,

You continue to look to Him for guidance, by conquering me.

Remember:

It is for this reason, that I long to once again come upon you,

So that you may remember to continuously give Him Praise.

However, if you choose to forever remain with the Lord,

Well that's good enough for me.

That way, I just simply fade away.

P75. "Born In War: Poems of Peace"

Poems of Wisdom/ J. Ellison

VIII. Poem V//

Understand, Understood

Understand there is not a single thing that can separate you from your dreams, understood.

Then understand there is no reason to not understand, if what you seek to understand has already been understood.

So understand it is universally understood that one decides to simply just "Tell it like it is" in understanding.

To help those others understand, even those lost understood, that they should understand in order to be found.

It seems understood, that GOD is greater than all things created, which some come to understand. However, to fully understand what is truly understood, one must understand the initial understanding.

I hope you understood, because understand this life can become very misunderstood and demanding.

Though have no worries, for the Lord understands everything understood in understanding.

Simply put, because it is understandingly of His Planning.

P76. "Born In War: Poems of Peace"

Poems of Wisdom/ J. Ellison

VIII. Poem VI//

The Wise Promise

I must learn to not judge others,

For I am not above judgement myself.

I must understand not to correct another's actions, without correctly addressing my own first.

I must persevere not to become a hypocrite, while teaching others in the Holy Word.

I must know that one day I will be judged myself, and by my spoken words I could become convicted.

I must walk daily as the Lord Guides me,

For if not, whom shall I help guide?

I must learn to ignore all urges to sway me from the Lord, and instead live to empower others,

For the Lord Himself, is greater, and

His Grace unparalleled fully covers.

I must be mindful of my thoughts regarding others, even when they think ill of me,

I make this promise to the Lord, with Him I shall remain eternally,

For it is He who remains dutifully with me.

P77. "Born In War: Poems of Peace"

Poems of Wisdom/ J. Ellison

VIII. Poem VII//

Parables I

He who is content in his earthly ways and rich in abundant treasures,

Is truly poor in the eyes of Heaven.

He who does not love those of his own household,

Has not learned the meaning of true love.

He who is quick to challenge GOD,

Becomes the first into destruction.

He who lives a Holy Life,

Becomes a treasure in the sight of GOD.

He who fights for GOD in his heart,

Can never truly become defeated.

He who loves money over all else,
Cannot truly be of GOD's heart.

He who preservers for GOD's sake,
Will gain everything once lost.

He who loves GOD more than anything of man,
Are the truest children of GOD.

He who walks with GOD,
Becomes he who remains with GOD.

For GOD has ordained us all into His Eternal Love,
A love that needs no token.

He Guides us as we were meant to be,
A Truth not easily spoken.

But He Grace is living,
His Heart is true,

He knows the True Awoken.

Though this world may fall,

This sea may shrivel,

His Love remains unbroken.

P78. "Born In War: Poems of Peace"

Poems of Wisdom/ J. Ellison

VIII. Poem VIII//

The Power of a Moment

Every step made is a step closer to You and Your Holy Kingdom.

Every word spoken is the building block towards a person's character.

Every moment has the potential to become a fond memory.

Every smile offers a glimpse into the eternal Joy of Heaven.

Remember this lesson,

Every second one day becomes a minute,

That minute once grown becomes an hour,

That hour at some point measures into a day,

Therefore, every second blossoms into eternity.

My friends,

Do not underestimate the power of the second.

Always Remain Grateful.

P79. "Born In War: Poems of Peace"

Poems of Wisdom/ J. Ellison

VIII. Poem IX//

Innocence of Child

The child is full of joy. The child represents innocence.

The child views the world as it was meant to be according to GOD's true design.

The child's laughter brightens the day of all.

The child's cry softens the heart of the World.

The child loves unrestricted. The child dreams while he is awake.

The child learns by growing from his mistakes.

The child seeks to repair and build those people broken around him.

The child worries not about money, but rather, genuine love given and received.

The child's actions can teach the actions of the adult,

It is for this reason that the adult should listen to the unspoken lesson of the Child.

For in the Child, GOD's true wisdom is revealed.

P80. "Born In War: Poems of Peace"

Poems of Wisdom/ J. Ellison

VIII. Poem X//

Find The Hidden Fruit

Every obstacle has it's prize.

Every challenge has it's reward.

For just as the muscle is torn in order for it's fibers to become stronger,

One's weakness is developed in order for their whole body to become stronger.

Every mountain has it's end,

Whereas every hill has it's beginning.

For just as we all must start somewhere to become one day great,

One must be brave enough to actually start that journey,

In order for those dreams to continue taking shape.

Every mind has it's own design,

Just as every hand has it's fingerprint.

Let us not strive to mimic others for the sake impressing others,

But rather, walk as the Creator intended for the sake of saving all others.

Though some pearls may be hidden,

They reveal great awe once finally found.

For some rewards are well worth the wait,

However, if you give up, they won't be found.

For what good is it to gain the world,

When you forfeit the Holy Crown?

For know the Lord is True at heart,

In Him we each have Life abound.

IX. POEMS OF JOY

P81. "Born In War: Poems of Peace"

Poems of Joy/ J. Ellison

IX. Poem I//

Freely Chained

Though we are freely given choice,
We are unknowingly chained.
We can reach to any bounds,
But are confined to the ring.
We create our own rules,
But must stay placed in the game.

By my oh my, what a joy!
To be released from those chains!

Though we move up in the world,
We are hindered in gain.

Though some claim to know it all,

They are slaves in the same.

We are slow to know the truth,

But we are quick to chase fame.

By my oh my, what a joy!

To be released from those chains!

When smoke and mirrors cloud our path,

Go decipher that maze.

When the world threatens in wrath,

Fight to rise through that pain.

Yes, the sky may downpour,

But grow to fight through that rain.

Cause my oh my, what a joy!

To know release from those chains!

P82. "Born In War: Poems of Peace"

Poems of Joy/ J. Ellison

IX. Poem II//

Near Me Control

Please Place Your Will in my heart Lord,
My Father Reside in my soul!
Dear Father I cherish Your Every Thought,
May dreams of You Near Me control.

My Father Lift in me my enemies,
May all those who know You behold!
For all is forgiven inside Your Love,
May thoughts of You Always know growth.

Dear Father Show In Me Your Qualities,
May all You Provide make us whole!
For all things are possible in Your Grace,
I pray You Wake in me Your Goal.

Forever we enter Your Joy Lord,

Forever Your Honor will hold!

For in You Is captured all memories,

In You every path forms a road.

P83. "Born In War: Poems of Peace"

Poems of Joy/ J. Ellison

IX. Poem III//

Be Graced In Spirit

If the sky has begun to fall,
Be graced it doesn't quicken.
If the rivers floods today,
Be graced that your a swimmer.
If a second passed in sigh,
Be grateful for that second.
For to joy in GOD's Hope,
Can lighten any ending.

When plans begin to fail,
Be graced to start anew.
If somehow you lose your job,
Be graced that work is through.
Found your timing's off in scope,
Be grateful for the clue.

For to joy in GOD's Hope,

Can lighten any mood.

Though people come and go,

Be graceful in their move.

Though the water slowly dries,

Be graceful for it's groove.

When a harm reveals its face,

Be graceful for the it's proof.

For to joy in GOD's Hope,

Can lighten any truth.

P84. "Born In War: Poems of Peace"

Poems of Joy/ J. Ellison

IX. Poem IV//

With Joy

I will stand with joy in my heart!
Through everything trying tear to me apart!
I will walk through the river,
I will storm through the terror.

I'll endure through forever,
With His Joy, I'll endeavor!

I will fight with love in my heart!
I will persist through the dimmest of dark!
I will push through those shivers,
To survive through that winter.

I'll endure through forever,
With His Joy, I'll endeavor!

I will live with joy in my heart!
Never quit, placed my eye on the course!
I will march through the splinters,
Run and dash as a sprinter.

I'll endure through forever,
With His Joy, I'll endeavor!
I will STAND with joy in my heart!

P85. "Born In War: Poems of Peace"

Poems of Joy/ J. Ellison

IX. Poem V//

Nothing You Must Do

There is nothing you must do,
To earn His True Love in His View.

He was born into the World,
To remove all sin and every bruise.

Know He sacrificed Himself,
So that He May save you.

There is nothing you must do,
Except, know Him in the Truth.

All forgiveness is extended,
All you need to do is reach.

Never pay one for a blessing,
All you need is true belief.

Just accept Him and be saved,
It's that simple, yes for each.

There is nothing you must do,
Except, learn Him in the Truth.

Through His Sacrifice we live,
All you have do give,
Every hope unto the Father,
For He Freely Hands the gift.

Yes, we've already been lifted!
Thank the Father from the Spirit!
There is nothing you must do,
Except, take Him in all Truth.

P86. "Born In War: Poems of Peace"

Poems of Joy/ J. Ellison

IX. Poem VI//

Thank The Father From Spirit

I have Life inside my dreams,
Though I've thought in strain.

I have Life inside my limbs,
Though I've walked in pain,

I have Life inside my body,
Though my movements are choppy.

I have Life inside my feet,
Though my shoes are flopping,

Thank the Father from Spirit,
He Is our saving Grace!

Praise and joy unto the Lord!

His Ways are truly great!

Lift the Father in all glory!

He prepares for us our place!

Give the Father every honor!

For the sleep He Makes Awake!

I have Life inside my feet,

To thank the Father in the rain.

I have Life inside my body,

To give Him all the praise.

I have Life inside my limbs,

To stretch forth all His Ways.

I have Life inside my dreams,

To witness all His Grace.

Thank the Father from Spirit,

He Is our saving Faith!

Praise and joy unto the Lord!
His Ways are truly great!

Lift the Father in all glory!
He prepares for us our place!
Give the Father every honor!
For the sleep He Makes Awake!

P87. "Born In War: Poems of Peace"

Poems of Joy/ J. Ellison

IX. Poem VII//

You Were, Are, and Will Be There

From the beginning of civilization,

You Have known us!

From the creation of the constitution,

You Have inspired us!

From the construction of the first building,

You Have empowered us!

From before the first breath, and before the first thought.

You Have known us!

Because You Were.

Into the Truth of Christ,

You Give us!

Into the righteousness of Your Word,
You Strengthen us!

Into the Holy Mindset,
You Challenge us!

Into Your Grace, and into Your Faith,
You Build us!

Because You Are.

Of Your True Purpose,
Comes our purpose!

Of Your Heart,
Comes our heart!

Of Your Ways,
Comes our way forward!

Of Your Ways,

We are renewed,

Of Your Ways we are sanctified!

Because You Are To Come.

For Indeed You Are, and Ever Shall Be!

Our Shinning Bright Light, clothed in all praise!

Please guide our lives throughout all our days!

Dear Father GOD, You Are Great Always!

P88. "Born In War: Poems of Peace"

Poems of Joy/ J. Ellison

IX. Poem VIII//

I Tell You The Truth

I say: "I can't."

He Says: "You Can."

I say: "Okay."

He Says: "I Tell You The Truth."

Then I say: "Why me?"

He Says: "Why Not?"

Then I say: "Okay."

He Says: "I Tell You The Truth."

I've been staring at this mountain,

Thinking this seems really big,

Overwhelmed by it's sheer nature,

Can I ever make a dent?

So I ponder then I pace some,

Then I wonder then I face up,
Towards the mountain, with my case of,
How can this move make sense?

So I think a million thoughts,
And I pray a million prayers,
For I know the Father Hears Me,
I'm not speaking just to stare.

So I walk up to the mountain,
Just to find a set of stairs,
Headed straight into the air,
Yes, the Lord Has Heard my prayer.

All because I said: "I can't."
He Said: "You Can."
I said: "Okay."
He Said: "I Tell You The Truth."

P89. "Born In War: Poems of Peace"

Poems of Joy/ J. Ellison

IX. Poem IX//

We Smile Regardless *:)*

Though some decide to not embrace us,
We smile regardless!
Though some taunt us towards our backs,
We *:)* regardless!
While some doubt the Holy message,
We smile regardless!

Our joy cannot be taken!
No, our faith cannot be shaken!

Though some call us bad names,
We smile regardless!
Though they bar us from events,
We *:)* regardless!

Though some stand against the Spirit,

We smile regardless!

Our joy cannot be taken!

No, our faith cannot be shaken!

Seek to crucify our names,

We smile regardless!

Choose to never hear us speak,

We *:)* regardless!

Claim our Lord is not the Christ,

We smile regardless!

Our joy cannot be taken!

No, our faith cannot be shaken!

For we smile, We *:)*, We smile regardless!

P90. "Born In War: Poems of Peace"

Poems of Joy/ J. Ellison

IX. Poem X//

SEEKLIFWJC

Strength to move a mountain.

Endurance to fight an army.

Empowerment to bolden thousands.

Knowledge to spread in learning.

Love unmatched in His Grace.

Inspiration to start the race.

Faith persisting throughout the journey.

Wisdom to know the pace.

Joy unmatched inside the Spirit.

Clarity to see the intent.

Though the message seems encrypted,

Plain sight can see restricted.

If one can pay attention,

The First Reveals the hidden.

All because He Gave us right,

To Seek Life With Jesus Christ.

X. POEMS OF CLARITY

P91. "Born In War: Poems of Peace"

Poems of Clarity/ J. Ellison

X. Poem I//

A Poem to Dad

You were there for me when I was broken.

You taught me the ways of the world, and how to survive.

You comforted me through those terrible nightmares.

You gave me strength, though I cried,

You wiped my nose though it continued bleeding night after night.

You told me, "I could be anything I want."

You told me, "Ignore those who doubt me."

You were kicked out of apartments for things we did as children.

You put up with us, though we were considered very bad children to most.

You remained strong for us, though others broke our

hearts again and again.

You taught us to become a family. You taught us to always love.

Though at one point I was on the wrong path,

You didn't abandon me, instead you gave up everything to reestablish me.

You were there when we lost our loved ones and so so many more.

You told us, "This life is what we make it."

You told us, "You would always be with us to the end."

So I thank you now Dad for your great accomplishments.

You were always there to set me free.

Though the world may not know you,

You are more important than that world to me.

□

P92. "Born In War: Poems of Peace"

Poems of Clarity/ J. Ellison

X. Poem II//

Invisible Chains

Go out and fly little bird,
Soar in the sky and be free,
But nevermind this little chain,
It only seeks to keep you from becoming all you can be.

Go out and sing beautiful bird,
Let your vocals echo through the seas,
But nevermind this little chain,
It only seeks to keep you from reaching your song key.

Go and conquer the mountains little bird,
Climb as high as you can see,
But nevermind this little chain,
It only seeks to keep you from those dreams.

Go become great little bird,

Let your dreams come to seed,

But nevermind this little chain,

It seeks to keep you from becoming all you can be.

For many have invisible locked chains attached,

Which seek to keep them from seeing.

However, the your true strength lies inside Him,

And it is there that you will find that lost key.

P93. "Born In War: Poems of Peace"

Poems of Clarity/ J. Ellison

X. Poem III//

Role Model

Sweet Child, You are my role model.

You see the joy in life, the way GOD originally designed.

You play in the wind as if you haven't a care in the world.

You eat happily cause you can, though your parents may be poor.

You give without expecting something to be given in return.

You have learned to love without end, though that love could one day cause your heart pain.

You constantly smile in the summer sun, though you are fully aware there's no shade.

You motivate me to grow as a person, as you become wiser with age.

You push me to continue in life, even when my hope seems to fade,

GOD Designed me to serve you in happiness,

Through all of my days,

My sweet child you are truly my role model in so many ways.

P94. "Born In War: Poems of Peace"

Poems of Clarity/ J. Ellison

X. Poem IV//

Redeemed I Stand

I renounce all that is evil.

I believe Jesus Christ died on the Cross for our sins.

I accept Him now as my Lord and Savior.

It is for this reason, I stand redeemed.

I renounce everything within me that is not of GOD.

I believe in Him and that I can not be conquered for His Sake.

I accept His Will for me now and forever.

So always, I stand redeemed.

I renounce the ways of the world.

I believe I have been granted eternal Life.

I accept that I am nothing without Him.

Therefore, I truly stand redeemed.

I renounce all negative thoughts.

I believe He who is in me is stronger than he who is in the World.

I accept that I am chosen child of Christ.

Into forever, so shall I stand redeemed.

I renounce the opinions of others concerning me.

I believe the Holy Father empowers me.

I accept that He is in total control of everything concerning me.

Because I stand redeemed.

I renounce every battle fought against me.

I believe every fight has already been won in Him.

I accept that victory in Christ's Name.

So now fiercely, I stand redeemed.

I renounce every bond that evil has had over me.

I believe that You Alone are our true GOD and Father.

I accept Jesus Christ now into my life to always use me as He Sees fit.

Because eternally, I stand redeemed.

To all, seek the Father, with all that is you.

Believe His Words with all your heart and soul.

Accept that He has truly erased your sins.

So that His Love may enter eternally unto you.

My Friends, then so shall it forever remain,

That We Stand Redeemed.

P95. "Born In War: Poems of Peace"

Poems of Clarity/ J. Ellison

X. Poem V//

Spirit Anewed

The old me would become angry once I failed at a task,

The new me would thank GOD for the opportunity.

The old me would hide my true self behind a mask,

The new me would embrace that truth in its purity.

The old me wouldn't care if my enemies hearts were broken,

The new me would seek every way to help them mend that pain.

The old me wouldn't mind if another became chastised for becoming too outspoken.

The new me would rather suffer first than see another suffer in vain.

It is for this reason that our old ways must become shed,

In order to carve room for those ways of the new.

Truthfully speaking, the old me would hate the new me instead,

But the new me would love the old me just as He Loves each of you!

P96. "Born In War: Poems of Peace"

Poems of Clarity/ J. Ellison

X. Poem VI//

Turn Instead To GOD

When one voice dictates you to choose revenge over love,

Choose instead the Father.

When one voice orders you to choose between your faith or worldly wrath,

I tell you, choose instead the Father.

Though you face ridicule, to choose between family and friends,

Choose instead the ways of the Holy Father.

While you face constant choice between despair and hopelessness,

Continue on, but choose instead the ways of the Holy Father.

For the decisions made on earth, are what sets our place

on the table of eternity.

The ways of the Holy Father are eternal.

The ways of those in the world are slowly passing away.

Never give up that which is eternal, for that which is temporary.

Whenever those problems of the world, began to overflow and beckon for your attention,

I tell you dear child,

It is then, that you should firmly choose instead the Father.

P97. "Born In War: Poems of Peace"

Poems of Clarity/ J. Ellison

X. Poem VII//

Who Better

For who better to become a leader in battle,

Than a person who cherishes peace.

Who better to become a leader of people, than the one who first begun as their servant.

Who better to change ways of that world,

Than those born originally of that world.

Who better to know the heart of the Living Father,

Than those truly born of the Father's Heart.

Who better to change all hearts and minds,

Than those of truly changed hearts and minds.

Is not true wisdom is better hidden in the lost,

For once found, their wisdom has grown for the sake of being once lost.

Therefore, rejoice in your trials,

For the Lord increases your wisdom through each obstacle presented.

P98. "Born In War: Poems of Peace"

Poems of Clarity/ J. Ellison

X. Poem VIII//

Into A New Creation

No problem before me is greater than You.

You Lift me up in spirit,

I hear the Angels sing.

You Show me the fountain of Life.

It's waters flow of happiness,

It's springs overflow of joy.

In You my air is love.

You Make my body as a feather,

My heart lifts with excitement.

You Lift the burden upon me.

I have never felt so free,

I now walk as a new creation,

To honor the Christ in me.

P99. "Born In War: Poems of Peace"

Poems of Clarity/ J. Ellison

X. Poem IX//

As We Were Meant To Be

Do not worry about what the next person does,
Nor let their accomplishments bury you.

Never let opinions tear you down,
Nor let one's status worry you.

Do not judge yourself against their standards,
Nor let peer pressure hurry you.

Do not let go of ambitions,
Nor let them come to burden you.

Do not follow unholy ways,
Nor let them stop your servitude.

You weren't meant to be as everyone,
That's why your chose from multitudes.

As we are, we were meant to be,
Designed uniquely of the Merciful.

Be joyed in who you currently are,
For GOD Created you purposeful.

P100. "Born In War: Poems of Peace"

Poems of Clarity/ J. Ellison

X. Poem X//

Hear Him Speak

Our Father Does Speak to us all,
To each in their various ways.

Our Father Lives in forgiveness,
He Gives and Takes Away.

Our Father Is pure in Spirit,
He Raises us away from sin.

Our Father Has loved us always,
He Reconciles us till the End.

Our Father Is pained when we doubt Him,
For it is He Who has created all things.

Our Father Spoke All in creation,

It is He Who Placed in you your dreams.

Our Father Walks close with the faithful,

He Is pleased when we each call His Name.

Our Father Delights in our happiness,

Though He Knows the struggles we've seen.

Our Father Gives all different blessings,

For He Knows our needs are unique.

Our Father Has Rendered Protection,

For He's Seen the danger beneath.

Our Father is high in Glory,

Though He Pleasures to wash our feet.

Our Father Loves His Children,

Through the world, we can hear Him Speak.

ABOUT THE AUTHOR

I was born in Andalusia, Alabama. I was raised by my father and met my beautifully humble mother later in life. I love both very dearly. Each are very beautiful people with genuinely gentle hearts. At the age of 23, I joined the United States Army, where I currently serve. I received the inspiration to write this book during my deployment to Operation Inherent Resolve. During my ten years in the military, I've traveled all over the world, deployed four times, met my beautiful wife (Olesja), and had three beautiful kids (Julian, Ariana, and Amariah). I became an author after giving my life to Jesus Christ and becoming saved. Best Decision Ever!

May the Peace of GOD be upon each of you always. My goal will always be to help in encouraging others while working to spread His Message to all people around the world. "Remember, no matter have far you've come, always continue further in Christ". #Dreambuilder

www.ingramcontent.com/pod-product-compliance
Lightning Source LLC
Chambersburg PA
CBHW031316040426
42443CB00005B/98

* 9 7 8 0 6 9 2 7 5 0 7 6 6 *